DATE DUE

FEB 09 2006			
FEB 1 0 2007		MAR 1 3 2014	
MAY 1 1 2009		JUN 0 2 2015	
JUN 0 8 2009			
FEB 0 9 2010			
FEB 1 8 2010			
APR 2 9 2010			
FEB 0 9 2012			
JAN 2 9 2013			
GAYLORD			PRINTED IN U.S.A.

Great African Americans

Martin Luther King, Jr.

man of peace

Revised Edition

Patricia and Fredrick McKissack

Enslow Publishers, Inc.

40 Industrial Road   PO Box 38
Box 398   Aldershot
Berkeley Heights, NJ 07922 Hants GU12 6BP
USA   UK

http://www.enslow.com

Revised edition of *Martin Luther King, Jr.: Man of Peace* © 1991

Library of Congress Cataloging-in-Publication Data

McKissack, Pat, 1944–
     Martin Luther King, Jr.: man of peace/Patricia and Fredrick McKissack — Rev. ed.
          p. cm. — (Great African Americans)
     Includes index.
     Summary: Simple text and illustrations describe the life and accomplishments of the revered
civil rights pioneer.
     ISBN 0-7660-1678-1
     1. King, Martin Luther, Jr., 1929–1968—Juvenile literature. 2. Afro-Americans—Biography—Juvenile
literature. 3. Civil rights workers—United States—Biography—Juvenile literature. 4. Baptists—United
States—Clergy—Biography—Juvenile literature. 5. Afro-Americans—Civil rights—History—20th
century—Juvenile literature. [1. King, Martin Luther, Jr., 1929–1968. 2. Civil rights workers. 3. Clergy.
4. Afro-Americans—Biography.] 1. McKissack, Fredrick. II. Title. III. Series.
     E185.97.K5 M363   2001
     323'.092—dc21

                              00-012150

Printed in the United States of America

10 9 8 7 6 5 4

To Our Readers:
We have done our best to make sure all Internet addresses in this book were active and appropriate when we
went to press. However, the author and the publisher have no control over and assume no liability for the
material available on those Internet sites or on other Web sites they may link to. Any comments or suggestions
can be sent by e-mail to comments@enslow.com or to the address on the back cover.

Every effort has been made to locate all copyright holders of material used in this book.
If any errors or omissions have occurred, corrections will be made in future editions of this book.

Illustration Credits: Alabama Bureau of Tourism & Travel, p. 15; Associated Press, p. 16T; Boston University,
pp. 17, 26; D.C. Public Library, p. 24; Library of Congress, pp. 3, 12, 14, 20, 21, 22, 27; Moorland-Spingarn
Research Center Howard University, p. 19; Morehouse College, pp. 10, 11; National Archives, pp. 4, 25; National
Park Service (National Historical Site), pp. 6, 7; Smithsonian Institution, p. 8.

Cover Illustrations: Boston University; D.C. Public Library; Library of Congress; Morehouse College; National
Archives.

TABLE of CONTENTS

Martin Luther King, Jr.

January 15, 1929–April 4, 1968

CHAPTER 1

Because You Are Colored

m artin Luther King, Jr., was born on January 15, 1929. He grew up in a big house on Auburn Avenue in Atlanta, Georgia.

Martin Luther King, Sr., was a Baptist preacher. Everybody called him Daddy King. He was a strong, proud man who taught his children to be proud also. Alberta King was "Mother Dear" to her three children.

Young Martin's family called him M.L.

Martin was born in this house in an African-American neighborhood in Atlanta.

But his friends called him "Tweed," because he wore tweed suits. His friends also called him "Will Shoot," because whenever the basketball was passed to him, he would shoot it.

There was also a serious side to Martin. He questioned segregation.

Segregation meant that black people were

treated differently from other people. Why did they have to ride on the back seats of buses? Use separate public bathrooms? And drink from different water fountains? Martin was told: *Because you are colored!*

As a boy, Martin worshiped at this church, where both his father and grandfather were pastors.

That's the way things were in the South when Martin was growing up. Once, Martin made a speech and won first place. He and his teacher rode the bus home. The bus filled up. So the driver told all the black riders that they had to give up their seats to

7

By law, Martin and other African Americans had to sit in the back on buses and trolley cars.

white passengers. When Martin asked why, he was told: *Because you are colored!*

Even though Martin Luther King, Jr., was young, he felt segregation was not a good way for Americans to live. Black and white people should have the same rights.

8

CHAPTER 2

Morehouse and More . . .

artin still had fun growing up. He loved the good soul-food meals prepared by his grandmother. He did so well in school that he graduated from high school when he was only fifteen. In the fall of 1944, he entered Morehouse College in Atlanta.

What was Martin going to be? Daddy King said he should be a preacher. Martin wasn't so sure about that. He was still very young. He had a lot

Martin, front row, third from left, attended chapel services for students at Morehouse College.

of questions about people, God, and what he would do in life.

A very important person in his life during that time was Dr. Benjamin Mays, the president of Morehouse. Dr. Mays was a very good friend and helped Martin look for his own answers.

By the time he finished Morehouse in the class of 1948, Martin knew he wanted to be a preacher. So he went to Crozer Theological Seminary in Chester, Pennsylvania.

At Crozer, Martin read about Mohandas Gandhi, who helped India gain freedom from England—peacefully. Martin also read the writings of Henry David Thoreau,

As a college student, Martin played on the football team and sang in the glee club. He graduated from Morehouse in 1948.

who said unfair laws should not be obeyed. Martin studied the words of Jesus and other holy leaders. His studies helped him find ways to fight prejudice peacefully.

There was racial prejudice in the North as well as in the South. But whenever it came up, Martin handled it peacefully. His classmates looked up to him, and even his enemies became his friends.

Love and peace were becoming very important words in Martin Luther King, Jr.'s life.

Martin admired Ghandi, a famous leader in India. Ghandi believed in finding peaceful ways to solve problems.

CHAPTER 3

Peaceful Protest

fter finishing Crozer Seminary in 1951, Martin went to Boston University. While living in Boston, Martin met Coretta Scott from Alabama. She was studying music at a school in Boston.

After their first date, Martin asked Coretta to marry him. She thought he was joking, but he wasn't. "She was everything I wanted in a wife," he told his best friend. And on June 18, 1953, Martin and Coretta were married.

Martin got his advanced degree in theology,

"I knew immediately that he was special," said
Coretta Scott when she met Martin. They had four children,
Yolanda, Martin III, Dexter, and Bernice.

and Coretta finished her studies, too. Then the
Kings had to decide where they would live. A
church in the South had asked Dr. King to come
there. Mrs. King wanted to stay in the North at
first. The South was still very segregated. But at
last, they decided to go back "down home."

In December 1954, the Reverend Dr. Martin Luther King, Jr., preached his first sermon as the pastor of Dexter Avenue Baptist Church in Montgomery, Alabama.

A year passed. It was December 1, 1955. An African-American woman named Rosa Parks got off from work and boarded a public bus. The bus filled, so she was asked to give up her seat to a white passenger. Mrs. Parks refused. At that time, it was against

Martin and Coretta named their son Dexter in honor of their first church— the Dexter Avenue Baptist Church.

15

the law for Mrs. Parks to refuse to give up her seat to a white person when the bus was crowded. So she was taken to the police station.

Black leaders in Montgomery called a meeting that evening at Dr. King's church. It was decided that a bus strike might help to change the unfair laws. Dr. King was asked to be the leader. He said he would, but only if the people taking part in the bus strike were peaceful.

For months and months, black people of Montgomery didn't ride the public buses. One year later, the bus company agreed to let all people, black and white, sit where they wanted.

After Rosa Parks refused to give her seat on a bus to a white person, she was arrested and fingerprinted.

16

Martin
Luther
King, Jr.,
was a
powerful
speaker,
and people
listened
to him.
"We will
not turn to
violence,"
he said.

CHAPTER 4

To the Mountaintop

a fter the Montgomery bus strike, Dr. King started the Southern Christian Leadership Conference (SCLC). He moved his family to Atlanta. Daddy King was very happy to have his son and family home again.

The South was changing. Young people were helping it happen. Students at North Carolina A&T University held peaceful sit-ins at segregated lunch counters.

Black and white students were working

At this sit-in at a whites-only lunch counter, some people tried to make trouble. They poured sugar, ketchup, and mustard over the heads of the protesters.

together to make America a better place. Black and white students formed a group under the SCLC known as the Student Non-Violent Coordinating Committee, or SNCC (pronounced "snick"). The group held sit-ins and peaceful protests all over the country. Americans were taking a stand against segregation—even if it meant they were beaten or put in jail. Dr. King was jailed many times, too. But he always said to stay peaceful.

In 1963, two well-known leaders, A. Philip Randolph and Bayard Rustin, planned the March on Washington for Jobs and Freedom. Other black leaders were asked to take part.

On a hot August morning in 1963, more than 250,000 people came to Washington, D.C., to the largest demonstration for rights ever held in this country! People came from all over the world in airplanes, trains, buses, and cars. Some walked, and some were carried. The large crowd was orderly and peaceful. They sang songs. A favorite was called "We Shall Overcome."

A. Philip Randolph was an organizer of the 1963 March on Washington.

In 1963, more than a quarter of a million people marched to the White House demanding civil rights.

Many people gave speeches that day. At the end of the long day, there was one more speaker: Martin Luther King, Jr.

He talked about having a dream where Americans lived in peace and friendship. "Let freedom ring," he said. And one day, he hoped all Americans might sing, "Free at last, free at last . . ."

"I have a dream," said Dr. King, who hoped that one day his four children would not be "judged by the color of their skin . . ."

CHAPTER 5

We Shall Overcome

f or his work, Dr. King was given the Nobel Peace Prize in 1964. He was the second African American to win this high honor.

President John F. Kennedy had pushed for laws that would protect the rights of all races. But he had been killed on November 22, 1963. President Lyndon B. Johnson wanted to work for equal rights, too. Dr. King was at the White House the day President Johnson signed the Voting Rights Act on August 6, 1965.

After receiving the Nobel Peace Prize, Dr. King posed for a portrait with his wife, Coretta, his parents, sister Willie Christine, and brother A.D.

Dr. King believed in peace. Some people didn't. They beat his followers. Churches were burned. Dogs and water hoses were turned on peaceful marchers. People were put in jail. Some were even killed. Many times people said they wanted to kill Dr. King.

Workers in Memphis, Tennessee, asked him to help them plan a peaceful march. Dr. King went to Memphis.

The march ended in violence. This bothered Dr. King very much. He wanted to hold another march. So he returned to Memphis.

24

The King family linked hands at the dinner table to say grace.

He stayed at the Lorraine Motel. On April 4, 1968, Martin Luther King, Jr., was killed by James Earl Ray. Ray served a life sentence in a Tennessee state prison. He died in 1998.

Mrs. Coretta King began the Center for Non-Violent Social Change, in Atlanta. People come from

Around the world, millions of people mourned the death of Dr. King.
This memorial service was held at Boston University.

all over the world to study Dr. King's life, writings, and peaceful demonstrations.

Today, long after Dr. King's death, he is a world hero loved by all people who dream and work for peace and freedom.

Today the birthday of Martin Luther King, Jr., is a holiday. Every year, on the third Monday in January, we honor his work and his dream. If his dream is remembered, then one day we might live together in peace.

timeLine

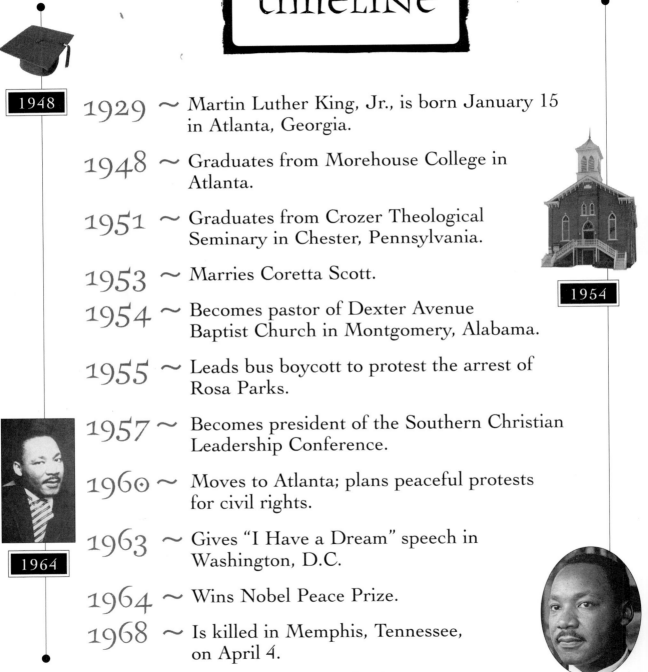

1948

1929 ~ Martin Luther King, Jr., is born January 15 in Atlanta, Georgia.

1948 ~ Graduates from Morehouse College in Atlanta.

1951 ~ Graduates from Crozer Theological Seminary in Chester, Pennsylvania.

1953 ~ Marries Coretta Scott.

1954 ~ Becomes pastor of Dexter Avenue Baptist Church in Montgomery, Alabama.

1955 ~ Leads bus boycott to protest the arrest of Rosa Parks.

1957 ~ Becomes president of the Southern Christian Leadership Conference.

1960 ~ Moves to Atlanta; plans peaceful protests for civil rights.

1963 ~ Gives "I Have a Dream" speech in Washington, D.C.

1964 ~ Wins Nobel Peace Prize.

1968 ~ Is killed in Memphis, Tennessee, on April 4.

1954

1964

WORDS to KNOW

colored—An outdated name for African Americans.

demonstration—A public showing of feeling for or against an issue.

Nobel Peace Prize—A special honor given to a person who works for peace in the world. It is named after Alfred Nobel, a man who left money in his will to start the prize.

nonviolent—Peaceful, without violence.

preacher—A teacher of religion.

prejudice—Dislike of people, places, or things without a good reason.

president—The leader of a country or group.

segregation—To keep people apart from one another because of race, religion, age, sex, or some other reason.

seminary—A school where religion is studied.

sit-in—A kind of demonstration; at the first sit-ins, blacks and whites sat at whites-only lunch counters waiting to be served. Later, sit-ins were used to object to different things, like war, poverty, and world hunger.

words to know

soul food—Food made popular by African Americans in the South; prepared in much the same way since the time of slavery.

students—People who attend a school.

theology—The study of religion.

tweed—A warm, heavy material made of different colors of wool woven together.

violence—Acts that hurt or destroy people, places, animals, and other things.

Learn more about Martin Luther King, Jr.

Books

Adler, David. *A Picture Book of Martin Luther King, Jr.* New York: Holiday House, 1996.

Bull, Angela, *Free At Last!: The Story of Martin Luther King, Jr.* New York: Dorling Kindersley, 2000.

Murray Peter. *Dreams: The Story of Martin Luther King, Jr.* Chanhassen, Minn.: Child's World, 1998.

Internet Addresses

MLK Online

Biography, photos, speeches
    <http://www.mlkonline.com/home.html>

The King Center

Learn more about Martin Luther King, Jr., and Coretta Scott King.
    <http://www.thekingcenter.com/mlk/bio.html>

"Martin Luther King, Jr."

Timeline, photos, soundclips.
    <http://seattletimes.nwsource.com/mlk>

King Papers Project

Timeline with links to photos, speeches, and more.
    <http://www.stanford.edu/group/King/>

iNdex